Lovers of The Storm

Lovers of The Storm

Anamika

PAPER TOWNS
PUBLISHERS

PAPER TOWNS
PUBLISHERS

First Published by
Paper Towns Publishers
72, Vishwanath Dham Colony,
Niwaru Road, Jhotwara,
Jaipur, 302012

Lovers of The Storm

ISBN Print Book -978-93-6185-511-5

Printed in India

For the ones in love with the night sky

Index

Lovers of The Storm

My mom asked me,
How could I ever love the storm?
Something so disastrous and unforgiving,
Something so unkind,
Kills everyone- dead or living.
But my heart wouldn't stop growing,
At the sight of the dark clouds,
When the thunder would scream out loud.
My pupils would dilate,
Witnessing the lightning.
The dead city illuminated,
By the divine energy.
It might scare the children,
And their guards,
But it ignites something pure in me.
Running like a maniac,
Often losing my balance,
I would reach the balcony,
And welcome the calamity home.
With open arms,

I would scream at the sky,
My mother witnessing the spectacle,
From across the dimly lit hall.
I let the beauty of the sight,
Devour my soul piece by piece.
There was a thrill.
The risk of getting blown away by its power.
Staring into the eye,
I let my guard slide lower and lower.
My mother's scream was muffled,
As she ran with staggering feet,
She was prepared for whatever came her way,
As long as she could protect,
Her precious little imbecile from it.
She had once known nature,
Just the way I tried to know it tonight.
She had known the glory,
And what came after.
She knows the compulsion,
And what it takes,
To fall in love with the danger.

The Warrior Princess

The silk drape flowing in the dark,
Her shoulders were carrying the sky on them,
With glitters and stars,
Sticking on her skin with sweat,
Courage oozing out of her.
Her long strides followed the light ahead.
Trapped inside her,
The shadows screamed as they burned,
Agony flowing through her veins,
Noises echoing in her ears.
She never looked back.
Pulled against the force of fear,
And the dreadful prospect of submission,
She used pain-
Her only source of determination.
It's all make-believe,
A terrible dream,
No longer to haunt her once she wakes up.
One step at a time,
She walked towards the engulfing moonlight.

The night grew heavy,
The mystery now dissolved in it.
In the cold winter night,
Now covered in rain-filled clouds,
Deafened by the silence of it,
The warrior princess,
Was nowhere to be found.

The First Letter

Three days ago,
It should've been here,
In the rain,
It was supposed to be drenched-
Smudging most of its ink,
The first letter to come from brother.
Close to his demise, he was,
That is what it means to be at war.
Death is so close,
That it is almost tangible,
Like a letter,
That the sisters and the mother awaited,
Longing for the proof of life.
The war is yet to begin,
There is still time,
It should be here any minute.
The rain must not stop,
The words are to come with it.
The family doesn't mind the lost words,
They mind losing their last shred of hope.

The son must come back,
Until then, the letters should do.
How important could it be,
An ugly, crumpled piece of paper,
Beaten by the weather,
Grabbed and trampled upon,
The sign of the soldiers being real,
Protecting their motherland,
And fighting the cruel.
Forget the flesh,
The land needs it.
With the rain,
Should come the letter,
The family awaits in terror.
The borders are miles away,
With the storm to stand guard.
With eyes heavy with tears and exhaustion,
The mother is now asleep,
And the sisters keep watch.
Wake her up! Wake her up!
Comes a distant voice,
Barefoot on the mud,

Covered in rain and urgency,
The boy came running and panting,
With a worn parchment in his hand.
Grabbed and torn, the name came into view.
The brother was fighting a war,
But peace came far at home.

The Lustrous Liquid

The partly clouded sky above your head,
The partly wet grass under your naked feet,
The droplets of rain, the hidden sun,
Aren't these enough to breathe in the sorrow and misery?
Let them lose themselves in your lungs filled with water.
Not the water you drink or take a shower with,
But the one you shed, just like the clouds do.

I pay no attention to the water dripping down your legs,
I am worried about the one rolling down your cheeks.
You become so clear when touched by the lustrous liquid,
That I can see the melancholy carved on your skin and your mind.
Those are not the marks of disobedience but endurance.

But remember one thing, the color red alone,

cannot make the rainbow.

I Am Not Ashamed

If only I had time, I would have breathed the light in,
For there was so much darkness I had within me.
My heart tried to keep you close, but couldn't.
Covered in all black, cocooned, my feelings were dying.
Holding the hand of your girl, you were passing by,
You caught me looking at you.
But probably didn't notice my longing for you,
For your love, your touch, for all of you I could ever have,
Although I knew it would never be enough.
I smiled.
Little did you know behind that smiling face was a heart, bleeding to death.
When you came close to me,
I shivered at the thought of losing the chance to hold you close.

For a moment, I forgot that I never even had a chance of anything,
But to watch you from far away,
Where the sunlight doesn't reach, you don't have promises to keep,
Where the moon doesn't glow at night and the knights don't have enemies to fight.
Being around the person you adore gives solace to the heart and soul, if not the flesh.
Warm water running down your naked body doesn't only touch the skin,
It touches your hidden desires.
I wanted you to touch me,
To feel your lips on mine, your chest against my breasts, your fingers around my neck and your hands on my waist.
But you had already chosen.
You had chosen a heart to love, one's wisdom to admire and flesh to smell.
But it wasn't mine. I could never be what you wanted me to be.

I don't see the lights anymore I once wished to breathe in,
I don't feel the air around me, the warmth of the sun,
Droplets of rain, beating of the heart, I don't feel any of it anymore.
Today, you are standing in front of me.
Crying, begging the last true friend of yours to come back to life.
I thank the almighty, but I can't.

A Promise to Keep

Tired legs and a tired mind,
Every movement of muscle,
Another tedious thing to get done tonight.
Just a few more yards,
A few more drags,
To let my body slump against the bed,
As I turn out the light.

But not before I let the water run,
Let it run all over my sweat-smeared skin,
As I rub the towel over my neck, chest and hair.
Fill my belly with the leftovers,
Just some salad and meat.
I feel my eyes burning now,
And with every passing second,
The night grows quieter.
The crickets and the passing cars,
The neighbours and their sporadic snores,
All too loud for what I crave.
It's just another day that I've survived,

Although it was just the same as my last one.
With a mind now numb,
and my sanity all lost,
I make the promise again to myself,
One more time.
A promise I need to keep,
"Tomorrow will nothing be like this",
With those words in my mouth,
and hope in my heart,
I listened closely to the rain now pouring,
As I closed my eyes to fall sound asleep.

<u>The Face, The Heart And The Soul</u>

Pretty is the face,
Of the one who desires,
The one who dares to dream,
Sing the song of the forbidden land,
Paint oneself with the colour of rebellion.

Brave is the soul,
of the one compassionate,
With empathy in their eyes,
And a smirk on the lips at all times,
The one who has no fear,
But only love to offer to the world.

Strong is the heart of the one,
of the one who endures,
Has failed time and time again,
Fell right on their face,
But got up with still the broadest of smiles,
Offered hands to the one in need,
At the dawn of desperate times.

The Portrait

She didn't desire to be looked so closely,
Certainly not by a stranger.
The painter at her door knocked with colours in his hands,
With pleading eyes, he asked,
But wasn't ready to be subjected to such an intense act.
He wanted to look at her,
And etch her features onto his now blank canvas.
Starting at her hairline,
and the forehead that followed,
Her eyebrows and in the middle where they met,
From the bridge of her nose,
To the very end of it.
Her eyes were filled with misery yet so bright,
They could blind you with but one glance.
Her pupils dilated at the sight of the painter,
He just wanted a chance.
Her lashes were like the curtains at the theatre,
The ones he visited last time he was here.

Her cheeks sunken with pale skin,
With marks of mystery,
Her lips blood red,
Turning brighter as she bit into them.
Her chin protruded,
Making way for the smoothness of her neck.

The shrug of her shoulders,
Shying away from the door.
But is it modesty or fear?
Fear of being known to the painter.
Oh, having to show herself and the vulnerability hidden.
He was honest and solemn,
And it's a beautiful city he came from,
But to her, he was a stranger just the same.

Let Me Go

You talked to the mood,
Said I don't believe that you believe in me.
You sing me a song,
My favourite of all,
Every night I cry,
To the moon about it.
You let your hair down,
And you don't even know,
You turn dust to life,
Getting us hypnotized.
Sensational is the world you live in,
Where all is forgiven,
Standing on the edge of it, I wait.
Ready to guard,
Ready to fail,
Ready to fall, if needed.
Deep, deep ocean eyes, I see,
I will drown if need be,
For you, I would count the stars in the sky,
Fly away with the birds,

Without even a good-bye,
Someday, look up at the blue,
And wonder if it was you,
The courage in your heart,
That made you finally let me go.

As Still As Water

The water is still,
Just like the pair of flapping wings,
Now calm somewhere deep within me,
My heartbeats dance,
To the occasional rippling of the serene liquid,
Not quite grey,
Not quite blue,
The momentary snapping of twigs above,
Distracting it can be,
But a reminder just the same.
Chaos is close.
Breathe in the humidity,
and let out the dubiety,
"For the one who protects can't be afraid."
So was I told,
By my old man a while ago,
Clenching my eyes shut one last time,
As all will be needed,
When I disrupt the forbidden peace,
With every passing drop,

A voice whispers the one thing I fear,
I, the warrior, can never be as still as water.

In Need Of A Dream

The air in me won't suffice,
I will need a lot more to survive.
I will need melody and poetry,
I will need a muse and tragedy,
I will need land beneath my feet,
And a sky above my head,
Two things so visible and divine,
And yet people choose to forget.
I will need a pair of wings,
To fly beyond all limits,
I will need the ocean,
And the calmness I find as I drown in it,
I will need the sound of the waves crashing against each other,
I will need warm breezes in the winter,
And cold showers in the summer,
I will need conspiracy and justified crimes,
I will need blood and blessings,
And let's not forget colors,
And walls full of paintings,

I will need fire to the unforgiving world down to the ground,
And I will need magic to bring it back to life.
I will need books,
And occasional visits to the shrines,
I will need age and time,
I will need a dream to be fully alive.

Smudges Beauty

The tears are still fresh,
And so is her sorrows.
Her kohl was smeared,
cheeks flushed but sunken,
With smudged spots of darkness,
And a tinge of something red.
Her lipstick had been messed with, too.
She was now a shade of maroon,
With agony carved on her skin,
And words stuck in her mouth.
She ran with a robe around her waist,
Climbed the stairs two at a time,
And let the faucet run
Splash! Splash! Splash!
Rub till all the colours are gone,
Rub till the skin's spotless,
Rub as long as there's still some left.
Marks aren't good, if you want a spotless image.
If you want to play the game,
Of building your own palace.

Self-Love

I look at the sky,
And it is grey.
I cannot say if it is cloudy enough,
But maybe it will rain.
I might not be fond of it,
But the sound of the raindrops makes me want to love myself,
A little more,
With every passing monsoon day.
Some make it look easy,
Make it sound easy,
It is easier said than done, I suppose,
For it's been twenty-one years,
And I still don't have a single photo.
With the pitter-patter of the water drops,
Echoing in my dull bedroom,
I grab hold of my notebook.
It smells of coffee and ink.
There's something else as well,
I just can't put a finger around it.

The fire was crackling when I looked up.
I had everything before the rain came,
But it felt like I had been waiting for days,
When it showed up.
It was a part of me,
And I didn't even know.
The thunder startled me,
Making me drop my book.
I looked closely,
Saw a paper sticking out,
Only today, I took a look.
A photograph.
Missing all the colours ,
Except for two or three, if you please.
I hope it's not too late,
To finally love myself,
Just the way I wish.

A Mindful Face

I saw another face,
Today at the train station.
It wasn't a distinctly pretty one,
But a decent one, set in motion.
Not so appealing,
I turned my head,
In search of beauty, amidst the ugly crowd,
I came across a few,
With fine eyes and thin lips,
But nothing that could hold my attention.

Then I saw the one.
The one I had been waiting for.
Dark hair and dark eyes,
Pointed nose and a charming smile.
This face had it all.
The story that never ends,
The painting that never fades.
He turned his head around,
And smirked at the kids around.

I went up to him and told him about my interest,
He looked around,
And then back at me again.
I assumed he would deny such a request,
But he doesn't know what he has been asked of.
He doesn't know about the ancient carvings on the walls,
He doesn't know about the stories that were told,
And the songs that were once sung.
I looked down at my hands,
Then back at him.
His face seemed to have aged,
Only in a few minutes.
It lost its elegance and youth.
Boy! It was a shame.
I smiled at him,
Trying not to mind his ignorance.
I looked around at the crowd again,
And began my search for a mindful face.

Do You Want To Read Something I Wrote

Do you want to read something I wrote?
It might be a little painful and cold.
It's about my fear, all my fears in one place,
Making me feel helpless,
And taking the breath out of my core.
They asked me to "chill",
Like my feelings aren't even valid.
I don't know if they are trying to help,
Or if this is what people call "gaslighting."
Well, here I am,
Swallowing my pride,
And finally letting my guard down,
I know it is getting late, and you should be home,
But before you go,
Do you want to read something I wrote?

The One In The Red Dress

The walls are grey,
And so are the people around,
They are all either black or white,
Not a single colour to be found,
It is considered outrageous,
To be yourself in a world always in a mask,
Keep it safe, keep it hidden,
That's the only significant task,
The task to be performed when you are within these walls.
The people don't understand how dire it is for them,
They are in desperate need of wake-up calls.
The grey walls are now cracking,
With the radiance of the one in colour,
The people are appalled,
But to her, none of it mattered,
The people talked and whispered about her,
"Is she a killer?", "Is she a sinner?"
But she was busy,

Making sure every eye was on her.
In a room full of black and white,
She was the only one in red.
They despised her for her confidence,
She was the kind to whom insecurities can't be fed,
People were uncertain of her future,
And dubious of her intentions,
But she did not make the appearance to impress,
She turned her head,
For one last look at the audience,
For she could only feel pity for them,
In a world full of dull, scornful people,
She was the girl in the red dress.

Too Young To Understand

I was four,
When I first heard of it,
War- the word terrifies me still.
I knew from the look on my father's face,
It couldn't be something good.
I was seven,
When I saw the bruises,
On my mother's arm,
When I asked, she would only say,
"It was an accident. Nothing to worry about".
I was ten,
When I saw my friend getting picked on,
For being a different race.
I was twelve,
When I noticed the growth in the length of my sister's skirt,
And the button around the collars of her shirt.
I was fourteen,
When I was told I was too young,
Too young for unforgiving racism,

For hostility and rendezvous with realism,
Too young to witness the bloodbath around me,
And all the positive criticism,
They said I was too young,
To understand when to keep my mouth shut,
And my eyes dry,
Too young to understand the value of silence and compromise,
To know what is safe,
And what might lead to my demise.
But it has all been done.
I have already seen the world as it is.
I wanted to tell them,
Scream at them,
The things they were telling me I didn't know how to do,
I had been doing them all my life.

The Sea and It's Eternity

With long strides, I walked,
The humid breeze keeping me company,
I am lost somewhere in my mind,
But also aware of the impending sight,
Of the water waves, waiting for no one,
I walked with gleam in my eyes,
And hope in my heart,
Is it finally my turn?
To witness the wonder,
To know it's infinite.
I walked,
Until the cold ocean water crashed against my ankles,
Taking a moment to believe my eyes.
There is truly no end to it.
No one knows where the sea ceases,
and where the sky begins.
My strides stared towards the ocean,
Not a care in the world.
The water crashed against my knees now,

Then against my hips,
Not long before it hit my neck and chest.
The taste of salt in my mouth,
And the burn in my eyes,
Made it all too real.
The sky and the sea,
The salt and the humid breeze,
The world and its entirety,
The life that was hidden somewhere deep within me.

Parallel Universe

With every turning page,
A new story to be told,
A new picture to behold,
A reader living a thousand lives,
Like one was never enough.
The reader is the warrior,
Sometimes the lover,
And sometimes the offender.
A taste so addictive,
To be allowed to finally become a nobody.
There's no cure, only withdrawal,
A dream,
Laced with the stench of leather and paper,
The sense of greed,
And the need to breathe,
All sewn together,
A sweet present for the reader.
The world has now been tuned out,
The screams and chaos of human existence,
Now fading into oblivion.

Now, in an alternate realm,
The reader is far from home,
Far from all responsibilities and expectations,
Living a life in his own parallel universe.

The Imposter

She was called a different name,
For she couldn't risk it all,
She couldn't let them know who she was,
Or what she truly wanted.
For she is supposed to be a commoner,
With no defence or armour,
Only her charm to protect her from the clamour,
Delighted in how she was playing the most
powerful men,
Confined in a room,
Relaxed and off their guards,
She poured the drinks in utter amusement.
What could a lady,
As delicate and powerless as her,
Could ever do to harm their business?
What could she ever do,
To make them want to grab for their guns,
And shoot in the distance,
She was only a temptation.
Amidst the spilling alcohol and crowd,

She was only a pretty bartender.
Flinching at every other sound,
However low, however loud,
She is no threat to the smugglers,
Or the most wanted killers.
She was there only to view it all,
To keep her eyes and ears open,
And mouth sealed shut,
At all times.
Not to look in the eye of the misters,
She kept her head down,
Avoiding all possible banters.
"Hey you, girl! Over here. We need drinks," came the sound,
From the posse behind,
She turned quickly as she flinched,
The men in question are mean,
And their remarks certainly snide.
Revealing the face,
Her hair blew in the air.
She looked at the one in the middle,
And that's when she knew,

She wasn't the only imposter.
Someone else was on the game, too.
But it was only harder now,
When she didn't know who was working with her,
And who was only acting to do so.

The Safety in Darkness

I clenched my eyes shut,
It is suddenly too bright in here,
I feel exposed and ready for consumption,
My skin tingles,
Under the blinding light in the room,
All my flaws, all my scars,
Out in the open for judgment.
I keep my eyes shut,
Hoping the stinging brightness will disappear,
And I can finally relax,
And be free of a caged mind,
Free of another sleepless night.
It can be hard to be patient,
When exhaustion is dripping all over you,
But with a mind, too alert to drift off to sleep,
Jumping out of my bed,
I walk with long strides.
I went across the room,
Blew the candles out and inhaled.
It was suddenly hard to tell where I was.

The mental map of my bed chamber,
Came to view in my mind.
I walked with small steps,
Let usavoid all possible collisions.
Once at the edge of the bed, I exhaled,
Tucked myself in,
My skin didn't sting anymore,
Nor was I scared f being seen.
The darkness might make me vulnerable,
But somehow, I still feel safe in it.

The Sea And You

Lying down with you,
On the wet sand,
Next to the never-ending blue.
There is something serene about it,
About you and these forbidden lands.
Embraced in your arms,
Feeling safe and content,
Happy and almost perfect,
Playing with your sand-soaked fingers,
The touch of your skin had an electricity to it,
But at the same time,
There was something intoxicating too.
I could hear the sea roaring
Somewhere far across,
Maybe jealous of what I have,
The protection and affection,
Friendship and devotion.
The simmering blur of blue and green,
The sun making the beauty glint in its light.
With darkness looming close ahead,

We only had a few moments of time.
But now my mind is dizzy,
And my heart giddy,
My skin warm against yours,
My eyelids are growing heavy.
We couldn't stay long,
Nor could we freeze time,
But a few more seconds,
I wouldn't mind.
So I closed my eyes,
Smelling the sea and salt lingering in the air,
Mixed with the sweet fragrance,
Of your golden brown flesh.
I swear I didn't do it on purpose,
But I fell asleep,
With your hand in my hand,
And name on my breath.

About the Author

Anamika was born in Kolkata, West Bengal, in 1998. She is an engineer and is currently working in Tata Consultancy Services. This is her first collection of poems, and is very close to her. She is a woman with a vision most people can't envision or fathom.